A
LITTLE BOOK
OF
NECESSARY NONSENSE

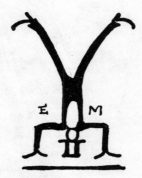

A LITTLE BOOK
OF
NECESSARY NONSENSE

Compiled by

Burges Johnson, 1877-1963, comp.

Illustrated by

Elizabeth MacKinstry

Granger Index Reprint Series

BOOKS FOR LIBRARIES PRESS
FREEPORT, NEW YORK

STANDARD BOOK NUMBER:
8369-6149-8

LIBRARY OF CONGRESS CATALOG CARD NUMBER:
72-116408

MANUFACTURED
BY
HALLMARK LITHOGRAPHERS, INC.
IN THE U.S.A.

vi

see p. v on reverse

Contents

v

see p. vi on reverse

Introduction

I saw a chubby little boy a-standing on his head.
It puzzled me to see him laugh (his face was very red).
I bade him stand as people should. He clapped his feet
  instead;
"You look so funny right-side-up, I have to laugh," he said.

IT IS not only little boys who every once in a while
would enjoy standing on their heads. A great
many solemn-faced grown-ups tire of being solemn
all the time and looking at the world right-side-up.
But they have gotten to be too stiff in the joints; and
many of them are too much afraid of what other
people might say.

Every healthy-minded person, big or little, wants
to be nonsensical now and then. If the big ones
are afraid to stand on their heads, or run around
in circles growling and squealing, they can at least
think nonsense. And some wise and great people
who have thought some of the funniest nonsense
have not been ashamed to write it down for other
sensible people to enjoy at the right moments.
Tennyson and Longfellow and Shelley and many
other poets have done it; William Makepeace
Thackeray, and Dr. Oliver Wendell Holmes wrote
a good deal. Dr. Samuel Johnson, who made a dic-
tionary, wrote some amusing foolishness in prose

ix

and verse; and so have great statesmen like William Pitt and John Hay.

If many wise authors have enjoyed writing a bit of nonsense now and then, you may be sure that very many more wise people have enjoyed reading it. That is why critics tell us that anyone who wants to become acquainted with the best English literature, old and new, must know something about the classics of nonsense.

This book is so little that it cannot bring together more than a very small part of the best. Perhaps it is better to include nothing but verse, and introduce you to prose nonsense at another time. But even so, it is hard to know what to put in and what to leave out. Edward Lear must be represented, of course. He is the king of them all. When John Ruskin made a list of the one hundred English books that everyone should read, he put Lear's Nonsense first. I have wanted to put in near the beginning some one of John Barham's "Ingoldsby Legends," but they are all too long. So you must find him out for yourself. Lewis Carroll (Charles Dodgson), who wrote *Alice in Wonderland* and *Sylvia and Bruno* must follow next. Like Lear, he wrote other more serious things, but the world has forgotten them, and remembers only the fun. William S. Gilbert, who wrote *Bab Ballads* and all the words for *Pinafore* and the other Gilbert and Sullivan operas, surely comes third.

But the best things from any one of these three alone would fill this book, and even then no two readers would agree with my choice. All I can do is to put in enough of their best to introduce each writer to you, if you do not already know him. And I must leave space here and there for a few other writers whose names you should know—even a few lines from some who are living and still writing—in the hope that you will think of this as no more than an introduction, and hurry to get better acquainted with them all.

BURGES JOHNSON

Acknowledgments

I wish to offer my sincere thanks and acknowledgment to the following authors who have been kind enough to give me personal permission to reprint their poems: to Carolyn Wells for poems reprinted from *Anthology of Nonsense*; to Oliver Herford for poems reprinted from *More Animals*; and to Gelett Burgess for poems reprinted from *Burgess Nonsense Book*.

BURGES JOHNSON

A
Little Book of
Necessary Nonsense

A
LITTLE BOOK
OF
NECESSARY NONSENSE

Here are a few bits of nonsense by famous writers whose names are known because of the serious things they published. Perhaps all of them wrote more nonsense than they ever put in books, to give pleasure to intimate friends!

Asleep, my Love?
What, dead, my dove?
O Pyramus, arise!
Speak, speak! Quite dumb?
Dead, dead? A tomb
Must cover thy sweet eyes.
These lily lips,
This cherry nose,
These cowslip cheeks,
Are gone, are gone:
Lovers, make moan:
His eyes were green as leeks.
O Sisters Three,
Come, come to me,
With hands as pale as milk;

Lay them in gore,
Since you have shore
With shears his thread of silk.
Tongue, not a word:
Come, trusty sword;
Come, blade, my breast imbrue;
And, farewell, friends,—
Thus Thisbe ends,—
Adieu, adieu, adieu.

William Shakespeare

As With My Hat

As with my hat upon my head
  I walked along the Strand,
I there did meet another man
  With his hat in his hand.

The tender infant, meek and mild,
  Fell down upon the stone;
The nurse took up the squealing child,
  But still the child squealed on.

Dr. Samuel Johnson

2

If a Man Who Turnips Cries

If a man who turnips cries
Cry not when his father dies,
'Tis a proof that he would rather
Have a turnip than a father.

Dr. Samuel Johnson

The Sailor's Consolation

One night came on a hurricane,
　The sea was mountains rolling,
When Barney Buntline turned his quid,
　And said to Billy Bowling:

"A strong nor'wester's blowing, Bill—
  Hark! don't ye hear it roar now?
Lord help 'em! how I pities all
  Unhappy folks on shore now!

"Foolhardy chaps who live in town—
  What danger they are all in,
And now are quaking in their beds,
  For fear the roof should fall in.

"Poor creatures! how they envies us,
  And wishes, I've a notion,
For our good luck, in such a storm,
  To be upon the ocean.

"Then as to them kept out all day
  On business from their houses,
And late at night are walking home
  To cheer their babes and spouses,

"While you and I upon the deck
  Are comfortably lying,
My eyes! what tiles and chimney pots
  About their heads are flying!

"And often have we seen or heard
  How men are killed or undone

5

By overturns in carriages
  And thieves and fires in London;

"We've heard what risks all landsmen run
  From noblemen to tailors,
So, Billy, let's thank Providence
  That you and I are sailors."

William Pitt

An Elegy on the Death of a Mad Dog

Good people all, of every sort,
  Give ear unto my song;
And if you find it wondrous short,—
  It cannot hold you long.

In Islington there was a man,
　Of whom the world might say
That still a godly race he ran,—
　Whene'er he went to pray.

A kind and gentle heart he had,
　To comfort friends and foes;
The naked every day he clad,—
　When he put on his clothes.

And in that town a dog was found,
　As many dogs there be,
Both mongrel, puppy, whelp, and hound,
　And curs of low degree.

The dog and man at first were friends;
　But when a pique began,
The dog, to gain some private ends,
　Went mad, and bit the man.

Around from all the neighboring streets,
　The wondering neighbors ran,
And swore the dog had lost his wits
　To bite so good a man.

The wound it seemed both sore and sad
　To every Christian eye;

7

And while they swore the dog was mad,
They swore the man would die.

But soon a wonder came to light,
That showed the rogues they lied;
The man recovered of the bite,
The dog it was that died.

Oliver Goldsmith

Little Billee

There were three sailors of Bristol City
Who took a boat and went to sea.
But first with beef and captain's biscuits
And pickled pork they loaded she.

There was gorging Jack and guzzling Jimmy,
And the youngest he was little Billee.
Now when they got as far as the Equator
They'd nothing left but one split pea.

Says gorging Jack to guzzling Jimmy,
"I am extremely hungaree."
To gorging Jack says guzzling Jimmy,
"We've nothing left, us must eat we."

Says gorging Jack to guzzling Jimmy,
"With one another we shouldn't agree!

There's little Bill, he's young and tender,
    We're old and tough, so let's eat he.

Oh! Billy, we're going to kill and eat you,
    So undo the button of your chemie."
When Bill received this information,
    He used his pocket handkerchie.

"First let me say my catechism,
    Which my poor mammy taught to me."
"Make haste, make haste," says guzzling Jimmy,
    While Jack pulled out his snickersnee.

So Billy went up to the main-top gallant mast,
    And down he fell on his bended knee.
He scarce had come to the twelfth commandment
    When up he jumps. "There's land I see:

"Jerusalem and Madagascar,
    And North and South Amerikee:
There's the British flag a riding at anchor,
    With Admiral Napier, K.C.B."

So when they got aboard of the Admiral's,
    He hanged fat Jack and flogged Jimmee;
But as for little Bill he made him
    The Captain of a Seventy-three.

William Makepeace Thackeray
10

There Was a Little Girl

There was a little girl,
And she had a little curl
  Right in the middle of her forehead.
When she was good
She was very, very good,
  And when she was bad she was horrid.

One day she went upstairs,
When her parents, unawares,
  In the kitchen were occupied with meals,
And she stood upon her head
On her little trundle-bed,
  And then began hooraying with her heels.

Her mother heard the noise,
And she thought it was the boys
  A-playing at a combat in the attic;
But when she climbed the stair,
And found Jemima there,
  She took and she did spank her most emphatic.

Henry Wadsworth Longfellow

Serenade

I'm a gay tra, la, la,
With my fal, lal, la, la,
And my bright—
And my light—
Tra, la, le.   (Repeat)
Then laugh, ha, ha, ha,
And ring, ting, ling, ling,
And sing, fal, la, la,
La, la, le.   (Repeat)

Bret Harte

The Ostrich Is a Silly Bird

The ostrich is a silly bird,
  With scarcely any mind.
He often runs so very fast,
  He leaves himself behind.

And when he gets there, has to stand
  And hang about till night,
Without a blessed thing to do
  Until he comes in sight.

Mary E. Wilkins Freeman

Sage Counsel

The lion is the beast to fight,
  He leaps along the plain,
And if you run with all your might,
  He runs with all his mane.
    I'm glad I'm not a Hottentot,
      But if I were, with outward cal-lum
    I'd either faint upon the spot
      Or hie me up a leafy pal-lum.

The chamois is the beast to hunt;
  He's fleeter than the wind,
And when the chamois is in front,
  The hunter is behind.
    The Tyrolese make famous cheese
      And hunt the chamois o'er the chaz-zums;
    I'd choose the former if you please,
      For precipices give me spaz-zums.

The polar bear will make a rug
  Almost as white as snow;

But if he gets you in his hug,
He rarely lets you go.
And Polar ice looks very nice,
With all the colors of a pris-sum;
But, if you'll follow my advice,
Stay home and learn your catechis-sum.

A. T. Quiller-Couch

*Edward Lear was born in England in 1812 and
died in 1888. He was a writer and artist, and be-
loved by many great men. Tennyson wrote a poem
to him, and Ruskin praised him. He wrote books
of travel and painted pictures that were exhibited at
the Royal Academy; but his books of nonsense,
illustrated by himself, were what really made him
famous.*

The Owl and the Pussy-Cat

The Owl and the Pussy-Cat went to sea
  In a beautiful pea-green boat:
They took some honey, and plenty of money
  Wrapped up in a five-pound note.
The Owl looked up to the stars above,
  And sang to a small guitar,
"O lovely Pussy, O Pussy, my love,
  What a beautiful Pussy you are,
      You are,
      You are!
  What a beautiful Pussy you are!"

II

Pussy said to the Owl, "You elegant fowl,
  How charmingly sweet you sing!

O! let us be married; too long we have tarried:
  But what shall we do for a ring?"
They sailed away, for a year and a day,
  To the land where the bong-tree grows;
And there in a wood a Piggy-wig stood,
  With a ring at the end of his nose,
      His nose,
      His nose,
  With a ring at the end of his nose.

III

"Dear Pig, are you willing to sell for one shilling
  Your ring?" Said the Piggy, "I will."
So they took it away, and were married next day
  By the Turkey who lives on the hill.
They dined on mince and slices of quince,
  Which they ate with a runcible spoon;
And hand in hand, on the edge of the sand,
  They danced by the light of the moon,
      The moon,
      The moon,
  They danced by the light of the moon.

                                        Edward Lear

The Dong with a Luminous Nose

When awful darkness and silence reign
Over the great Gromboolian plain,
Through the long, long wintry night;
When the angry breakers roar
As they beat on the rocky shore;
   When Storm-clouds brook on the towering heights
Of the Hills of the Chankly Bore,—

Then, through the vast and gloomy dark
There moves what seems a fiery spark,
   A lonely spark with silvery rays
   Piercing the coal-black night,—
   A Meteor strange and bright:
Hither and thither the vision strays,
   A single lurid light.

Slowly it wanders, pauses, creeps,—
Anon it sparkles, flashes, and leaps;
17

And ever as onward it gleaming goes
A light on the Bong-tree stems it throws.
And those who watch at that midnight hour
From Hall or Terrace or lofty Tower,
Cry, as the wild light passes along,—
    "The Dong! the Dong!
  The wandering Dong through the forest goes!
    The Dong! the Dong!
  The Dong with a luminous Nose!"

      Long years ago
  The Dong was happy and gay,
Till he fell in love with a Jumbly Girl
  Who came to those shores one day.
For the Jumblies came in a sieve, they did,—
Landing at eve near the Zemmery Fidd
      Where the Oblong Oysters grow,
  And the rocks are smooth and gray.
And all the woods and the valleys rang
With the Chorus they daily and nightly sang,—
  "Far and few, far and few,
  Are the lands where the Jumblies live;
  Their heads are green, and their hands are blue,
  And they went to sea in a sieve."

Happily, happily passed those days!
     While the cheerful Jumblies staid;
  They danced in circlets all night long,
19

To the plaintive pipe of the lively Dong,
        In moonlight, shine, or shade.
For day and night he was always there
By the side of the Jumbly Girl so fair,
With her sky-blue hands and her sea-green hair;
Till the morning came of that hateful day
When the Jumblies sailed in their sieve away,
And the Dong was left on the cruel shore
Gazing, gazing evermore,—
Ever keeping his weary eyes on
That pea-green sail on the far horizon,—
Singing the Jumbly Chorus still
As he sate all day on the grassy hill,—
    "Far and few, far and few,
        Are the lands where the Jumblies live;
    Their heads are green, and their hands are blue,
        And they went to sea in a sieve."

But when the sun was low in the West,
    The Dong arose and said,—
"What 'little sense I once possessed
    Has quite gone out of my head!"
And since that day he wanders still
By lake and forest, marsh and hill,
Singing, "O somewhere, in valley or plain,
Might I find my Jumbly Girl again!
For ever I'll seek by lake and shore
Till I find my Jumbly Girl once more!"

Playing a pipe with silvery squeaks,
Since then his Jumbly Girl he seeks;
And because by night he could not see,
He gathered the bark of the Twangum Tree
　On the flowery plain that grows.
　And he wove him a wondrous Nose,—
A Nose as strange as a Nose could be!
Of vast proportions and painted red,
And tied with cords to the back of his head.
In a hollow rounded space it ended
With a luminous Lamp within suspended,
　All fenced about
　With a bandage stout
　To prevent the wind from blowing it out;
And with holes all round to send the light
In gleaming rays on the dismal night.

And now each night, and all night. long,
Over those plains still roams the Dong;
And above the wail of the Chimp and Snipe
You may hear the squeak of his plaintive pipe,
While ever he seeks, but seeks in vain,
To meet with his Jumbly Girl again;
Lonely and wild, all night he goes,—
The Dong with a luminous Nose!
And all who watch at the midnight hour,
From Hall or Terrace or lofty Tower,
Cry, as they trace the Meteor bright,

21

Moving along through the dreary night,—
  "This is the hour when forth he goes,
The Dong with a luminous Nose!
Yonder, over the plain he goes,—
    He goes!
    He goes,—
The Dong with a luminous Nose!"

Edward Lear

The Yonghy-Bonghy-Bo

On the Coast of Coromandel
  Where the early pumpkins blow,
  In the middle of the woods
  Lived the Yonghy-Bonghy-Bo.
Two old chairs, and half a candle,
One old jug without a handle,
    These were all his worldly goods:
    In the middle of the woods,
    These were all the worldly goods
Of the Yonghy-Bonghy-Bo,
Of the Yonghy-Bonghy-Bo.

II

Once, among the Bong trees walking
  Where the early pumpkins blow,
    To a little heap of stones
    Came the Yonghy-Bonghy-Bo.
There he heard a Lady talking,
To some milk-white Hens of Dorking,—
  " 'Tis the Lady Jingly Jones!
    On that little heap of stones
    Sits the Lady Jingly Jones!"
  Said the Yonghy-Bonghy-Bo,
  Said the Yonghy-Bonghy-Bo.

III

"Lady Jingly! Lady Jingly!
  Sitting where the pumpkins blow,
    Will you come and be my wife?"
  Said the Yonghy-Bonghy-Bo,
"I am tired of living singly,—
On this coast so wild and shingly,—
    I'm a-weary of my life;
    If you'll come and be my wife,
    Quite serene would be my life!"
  Said the Yonghy-Bonghy-Bo,
  Said the Yonghy-Bonghy-Bo.

IV

"On this Coast of Coromandel
  Shrimps and watercresses grow,
    Prawns are plentiful and cheap,"
  Said the Yonghy-Bonghy-Bo.
"You shall have my chairs and candle,
And my jug without a handle!
    Gaze upon the rolling deep
      (Fish is plentiful and cheap):
    As the sea, my love is deep!"
  Said the Yonghy-Bonghy-Bo,
  Said the Yonghy-Bonghy-Bo.

V

Lady Jingly answered sadly,
  And her tears began to flow,—
    "Your proposal comes too late,
  Mr. Yonghy-Bonghy-Bo!
I would be your wife most gladly!"
(Here she twirled her fingers madly,)
    "But in England I've a mate!
    Yes! you've asked me far too late,
    For in England I've a mate,
  Mr. Yonghy-Bonghy-Bo!
  Mr. Yonghy-Bonghy-Bo!

VI

"Mr. Jones (his name is Handel,—
  Handel Jones, Esquire & Co.)
    Dorking fowls delights to send,
  Mr. Yonghy-Bonghy-Bo!
Keep, oh, keep your chairs and candle,
And your jug without a handle,—
    I can merely be your friend!
    Should my Jones more Dorkings send,
    I will give you three, my friend!
  Mr. Yonghy-Bonghy-Bo!
  Mr. Yonghy-Bonghy-Bo!

VII

"Though you've such a tiny body,
  And your head so large doth grow,—
    Though your hat may blow away,
  Mr. Yonghy-Bonghy-Bo!
Though you're such a Hoddy Doddy,
Yet I wish that I could modi—
    fi the words I needs must say!
    Will you please to go away?
    That is all I have to say,
  Mr. Yonghy-Bonghy-Bo!
  Mr. Yonghy-Bonghy-Bo!"

VIII

Down the slippery slopes of Myrtle,
  Where the early pumpkins blow,
    To the calm and silent sea
  Fled the Yonghy-Bonghy-Bo.
There, beyond the Bay of Gurtle,
Lay a large and lively Turtle.
    "You're the Cove," he said, "for me:
      On your back beyond the sea,
      Turtle, you shall carry me!"
  Said the Yonghy-Bonghy-Bo,
  Said the Yonghy-Bonghy-Bo.

IX

Through the silent roaring ocean
  Did the Turtle swiftly go;
    Holding fast upon his shell
  Rode the Yonghy-Bonghy-Bo.
With a sad primaeval motion
Toward the sunset isles of Boshen
    Still the Turtle bore him well,
    Holding fast upon his shell.
    "Lady Jingly Jones, farewell!"
  Sang the Yonghy-Bonghy-Bo,
  Sang the Yonghy-Bonghy-Bo.

X

From the Coast of Coromandel
　　Did that Lady never go,
　　　On that heap of stones she mourns
　　For the Yonghy-Bonghy-Bo.
On that Coast of Coromandel,
In his jug without a handle
　　　Still she weeps, and daily moans;
　　　On her little heap of stones
　　　To her Dorking Hens she moans,
　　For the Yonghy-Bonghy-Bo,
　　For the Yonghy-Bonghy-Bo.

Edward Lear

The Pobble Who Has No Toes

The Pobble who has no toes
　　Had once as many as we;
　　When they said, "Some day you may lose them
　　　all,"
He replied, "Fish fiddle de-dee!"
And his Aunt Jobiska made him drink
Lavender water tinged with pink;
For she said, "The World in general knows
There's nothing so good for a Pobble's toes!"

28

The Pobble who has no toes
   Swam across the Bristol Channel;
But before he set out he wrapped his nose
   In a piece of scarlet flannel.
For his Aunt Jobiska said, "No harm
Can come to his toes if his nose is warm;
And it's perfectly known that a Pobble's toes
Are safe—provided he minds his nose."

The Pobble swam fast and well,
   And when boats or ships came near him,
He tinkledy-binkledy-winkled a bell
   So that all the world could hear him.
And all the Sailors and Admirals cried,
When they saw him nearing the farther side,
"He has gone to fish for his Aunt Jobiska's
Runcible Cat with crimson whiskers!"

But before he touched the shore—
   The shore of the Bristol Channel,
A sea-green Porpoise carried away
   His wrapper of scarlet flannel.
And when he came to observe his feet,
Formerly garnished with toes so neat,
His face at once became forlorn
On perceiving that all his toes were gone!

And nobody ever knew,
  From that dark day to the present,
Whoso had taken the Pobble's toes,
  In a manner so far from pleasant.
Whether the shrimps or crawfish gray,
Or crafty mermaids stole them away,
Nobody knew; and nobody knows
How the Pobble was robbed of his twice five toes!

The Pobble who has no toes
  Was placed in a friendly Bark,

And they rowed him back and carried him up
  To his Aunt Jobiska's Park.
And she made him a feast at his earnest wish,
Of eggs and buttercups fried with fish;
And she said, "It's a fact the whole world knows,
That Pobbles are happier without their toes."

Edward Lear

The Jumblies

I

They went to sea in a sieve, they did;
  In a sieve they went to sea:
In spite of all their friends could say,
On a winter's morn, on a stormy day,
  In a sieve they went to sea.
And when the sieve turned round and round,
And every one cried, "You'll all be drowned!"
They called aloud, "Our sieve ain't big;
But we don't care a button, we don't care a fig:
  In a sieve we'll go to sea!"
    Far and few, far and few,
      Are the lands where the Jumblies live:
      Their heads are green, and their hands are blue;
      And they went to sea in a sieve.

II

They sailed away in a sieve, they did,
  In a sieve they sailed so fast,
With only a beautiful pea-green veil
Tied with a ribbon, by way of a sail,
  To a small tobacco-pipe mast.
And every one said who saw them go,
"Oh! won't they be soon upset, you know?
For the sky is dark, and the voyage is long;
And, happen what may, it's extremely wrong
  In a sieve to sail so fast."
    Far and few, far and few,
      Are the lands where the Jumblies live:
      Their heads are green, and their hands are blue;
      And they went to sea in a sieve.

III

The water it soon came in, it did;
  The water it soon came in:
So, to keep them dry, they wrapped their feet
In a pinky paper all folded neat;
  And they fastened it down with a pin.
And they passed the night in a crockery-jar;
And each of them said, "How wise we are!
Though the sky be dark, and the voyage be long,
Yet we never can think we were rash or wrong,

32

While round in our sieve we spin."
  Far and few, far and few,
    Are the lands where the Jumblies live;
    Their heads are green, and their hands are blue;
    And they went to sea in a sieve.

IV

And all night long they sailed away;
  And when the sun went down,
They whistled and warbled a moony song
To the echoing sound of a coppery gong,
  In the shade of the mountains brown.
"O Timballoo! How happy we are
When we live in a sieve and a crockery-jar!
And all night long, in the moonlight pale,
We sail away with a pea-green sail
  In the shade of the mountains brown."
  Far and few, far and few,
    Are the lands where the Jumblies live:
    Their heads are green, and their hands are blue;
    And they went to sea in a sieve.

V

They sailed to the Western Sea, they did,—
  To a land all covered with trees:

33

And they bought an owl, and a useful cart,
And a pound of rice, and a cranberry-tart,
  And a hive of silvery bees;
And they bought a pig, and some green jackdaws,
And a lovely monkey with lollipop paws,
And forty bottles of ring-bo-ree,
  And no end of Stilton cheese.
    Far and few, far and few,
      Are the lands where the Jumblies live:
    Their heads are green, and their hands are blue;
      And they went to sea in a sieve.

VI

And in twenty years they all came back,—
  In twenty years or more;
And every one said, "How tall they've grown!
For they've been to the Lakes, and the Torrible
    Zone,
  And the hills of the Chankly Bore."
And they drank their health, and gave them a feast
Of dumplings made of beautiful yeast;
And every one said, "If we only live,
We, too, will go to sea in a sieve,
  To the hills of the Chankly Bore."
    Far and few, far and few,
      Are the lands where the Jumblies live:

Their heads are green, and their hands are blue;
And they went to sea in a sieve.

Edward Lear

Limericks

There was once a man with a beard
Who said, "It is just as I feared!—
  Two Owls and a Hen,
  Four Larks and a Wren
Have all built their nests in my beard."

There was an old man in a tree
Who was horribly bored by a bee;
  When they said, "Does it buzz?"
  He replied, "Yes, it does!
It's a regular brute of a bee!"

There was an old man of Thermopylae,
Who never did anything properly;
  But they said, "If you choose
  To boil eggs in your shoes,
You shall never remain in Thermopylae."

There was an Old Person whose habits
Induced him to feed upon Rabbits;
   When he'd eaten eighteen,
   He turned perfectly green,
Upon which he relinquished those habits.

There was an Old Man who supposed
That the street door was partially closed;
   But some very large Rats
   Ate his coats and his hats,
While that futile Old Gentleman dozed.

There was an Old Man of Melrose;
Who walked on the tips of his toes;
   But they said, "It ain't pleasant
   To see you at present,
You stupid Old Man of Melrose."

Edward Lear

Lewis Carroll lived in England from 1832 to 1898. His real name was Charles Lutwidge Dodgson and he was a learned mathematician. But his many serious books are nearly all forgotten, while "Alice in Wonderland," "Through the Looking-glass," "Hunting of the Snark," "Sylvie and Bruno," "Rhyme and Reason?" will live as long as children and grown-ups love nonsense.

Jabberwocky

'Twas brillig, and the slithy toves
   Did gyre and gimble in the wabe;
All mimsy were the borogroves,
   And the mome raths outgrabe.

"Beware the Jabberwock, my son!
   The jaws that bite, the claws that catch!
Beware the Jubjub bird, and shun
   The frumious Bandersnatch!"

He took his vorpal sword in hand:
   Long time the manxome foe he sought.
So rested he by the Tumtum tree,
   And stood awhile in thought.

And as in uffish thought he stood,
   The Jabberwock with eyes of flame,

Came whiffling through the tulgey wood,
  And burbled as it came!

One, two! One, two! And through, and through
  The vorpal blade went snicker-snack!
He left it dead, and with its head
  He went galumphing back.

"And hast thou slain the Jabberwock?
  Come to my arms, my beamish boy!
Oh frabjous day! Callooh! callay!"
  He chortled in his joy.

'Twas brillig, and the slithy toves
  Did gyre and gimble in the wabe;
All mimsy were the borogroves
  And the mome raths outgrabe.

Lewis Carroll

Father William

"You are old, Father William," the young man said,
   "And your hair has become very white;
And yet you incessantly stand on your head—
   Do you think, at your age, it is right?"

"In my youth," Father William replied to his son,
   "I feared it might injure the brain;
But now that I'm perfectly sure I have none,
   Why, I do it again and again."

"You are old," said the youth, "as I mentioned be-
   fore,
   And have grown most uncommonly fat;

Yet you turned a back-somersault in at the door—
  Pray, what is the reason of that?"

"In my youth," said the sage, as he shook his gray
    locks,
  "I kept all my limbs very supple
By the use of this ointment—one shilling the box—
  Allow me to sell you a couple."

"You are old," said the youth, "and your jaws are
    too weak
  For anything tougher than suet;
Yet you finished the goose, with the bones and the
    beak:
  Pray how did you manage to do it?"

"In my youth," said his father, "I took to the law,
  And argued each case with my wife;
And the muscular strength which it gave to my jaw
  Has lasted the rest of my life."

"You are old," said the youth; "one would hardly
    suppose
  That your eye was as steady as ever;
Yet you balance an eel on the end of your nose—
  What made you so awfully clever?"

"I have answered three questions, and that is
    enough,"
  Said his father; "don't give yourself airs!
Do you think I can listen all day to such stuff?
  Be off, or I'll kick you down stairs!"

Lewis Carroll

He Thought He Saw a Banker's Clerk

He thought he saw a Banker's clerk
    Descending from the 'bus;
He looked again, and found it was
    A Hippopotamus.
"If this should stay to dine," he said,
    "There won't be much for us!"

He thought he saw an Albatross
    That fluttered round the lamp:
He looked again, and found it was
    A Penny-Postage-Stamp.
"You'd best be getting home," he said;
    "The nights are very damp!"

He thought he saw a Coach-and-Four
    That stood beside his bed:
He looked again, and found it was
    A Bear without a Head.

43

"Poor thing," he said, "poor silly thing!
  It's waiting to be fed!"

He thought he saw a Kangaroo
  That worked a coffee-mill:
He looked again, and found it was
  A Vegetable-Pill.
"Were I to swallow this," he said,
  "I should be very ill!"

He thought he saw a Rattlesnake
  That questioned him in Greek:
He looked again, and found it was
  The Middle of Next Week.
"The one thing I regret," he said,
  "Is that it cannot speak!"

Lewis Carroll

The Walrus and the Carpenter

The sun was shining on the sea,
  Shining with all his might:
He did his very best to make
  The billows smooth and bright—
And this was odd, because it was
  The middle of the night.

The moon was shining sulkily,
  Because she thought the sun
Had got no business to be there
  After the day was done—
"It's very rude of him," she said,
  "To come and spoil the fun!"

The sea was wet as wet could be,
  The sands were dry as dry.
You could not see a cloud, because
  No cloud was in the sky:
No birds were flying overhead—
  There were no birds to fly.

The Walrus and the Carpenter
  Were walking close at hand;
They wept like anything to see
  Such quantities of sand:
"If this were only cleared away,"
  They said, "it would be grand!"

"If seven maids with seven mops
  Swept it for half a year,
Do you suppose," the Walrus said,
  "That they could get it clear?"
"I doubt it," said the Carpenter,
  And shed a bitter tear.

45

"O Oysters come and walk with us!"
  The Walrus did beseech.
"A pleasant walk, a pleasant talk,
  Along the briny beach:
We cannot do with more than four,
  To give a hand to each."

The eldest Oyster looked at him,
  But not a word he said:
The eldest Oyster winked his eye,
  And shook his heavy head—
Meaning to say he did not choose
  To leave the oyster-bed.

But four young Oysters hurried up,
  All eager for the treat:
Their coats were brushed, their faces washed,
  Their shoes were clean and neat—
And this was odd, because, you know,
  They hadn't any feet.

Four other Oysters followed them,
  And yet another four;
And thick and fast they came at last,
  And more, and more, and more—
All hopping through the frothy waves,
  And scrambling to the shore.

46

The Walrus and the Carpenter
  Walked on a mile or so,
And then they rested on a rock
  Conveniently low:
And all the little Oysters stood
  And waited in a row.

"The time has come," the Walrus said,
  "To talk of many things:
Of shoes—and ships—and sealing-wax—
  Of cabbages—and kings—
And why the sea is boiling hot—
  And whether pigs have wings."

"But wait a bit," the Oysters cried,
  "Before we have our chat;
For some of us are out of breath,
  And all of us are fat!"
"No hurry!" said the Carpenter.
  They thanked him much for that.

"A loaf of bread," the Walrus said,
  "Is what we chiefly need:
Pepper and vinegar besides
  Are very good indeed—
Now if you're ready, Oysters dear,
  We can begin to feed."

"But not on us!" the Oysters cried,
  Turning a little blue.
"After such kindness that would be
  A dismal thing to do."
"The night is fine," the Walrus said,
  "Do you admire the view?"

"It was so kind of you to come!
  And you are very nice!"
The Carpenter said nothing but
  "Cut us another slice:
I wish you were not quite so deaf—
  I've had to ask you twice!"

"It seems a shame," the Walrus said,
  "To play them such a trick,
After we've brought them out so far,
  And made them trot so quick!"
The Carpenter said nothing but
  "The butter's spread too thick!"

"I weep for you," the Walrus said;
  "I deeply sympathize."
With sobs and tears he sorted out
  Those of the largest size,
Holding his pocket-handkerchief
  Before his streaming eyes.

"O Oysters," said the Carpenter,
  "You've had a pleasant run!
Shall we be trotting home again?"
  But answer came there none—
And this was scarcely odd, because
  They'd eaten every one.

Lewis Carroll

*William Schwenck Gilbert was also an English-
man who lived from 1836 to 1911. He was a de-
scendant of Sir Humphrey Gilbert, and himself be-
came a knight. He was a lawyer and a magistrate,
but he will always be remembered for his "Bab
Ballads" and for the operas he wrote with Sir Arthur
Sullivan.*

A Limerick in Blank Verse

There was an old man of St. Bees,
Who was stung in the arm by a wasp:
  When they asked, "Does it hurt?"
  He replied, "No, it doesn't,
But I thought all the while 'twas a Hornet!"

William S. Gilbert

The Story of Prince Agib

Strike the concertina's melancholy string!
Blow the spirit-stirring harp like anything!
  Let the piano's martial blast
  Rouse the Echoes of the Past,
For of Agib, Prince of Tartary, I sing!

51

Of Agib, who amid Tartaric scenes
Wrote a lot of ballet-music in his teens:
   His gentle spirit rolls
   In the melody of souls—
Which is pretty, but I don't know what it means.

Of Agib, who could readily, at sight,
Strum a march upon the loud Theodolite.
   He would diligently play
   On the Zoetrope all day,
And blow the gay Pantechnicon all night.

One winter—I am shaky in my dates—
Came two starving Tartar minstrels to his gates,
   Oh, Allah be obeyed,
   How infernally they played!
I remember that they called themselves the
   "Oüaits."

Oh! that day of sorrow, misery, and rage,
I shall carry to the Catacombs of Age,
   Photographically lined
   On the tablet of my mind,
When a yesterday has faded from its page!

Alas! Prince Agib went and asked them in!
Gave them beer, and eggs, and sweets, and scent,
    and tin.
    And when (as snobs would say)
    They "put it all away,"
He requested them to tune up and begin.

Though its icy horror chill you to the core,
I will tell you what
    I never told
        before,
    The consequences true
    Of that awful interview,
For I listened at
    the keyhole in
        the door!

They played him a sonata—let me see!
"Medulla oblongata"—key of G.
    Then they began to sing
    That extremely lovely thing,
Scherzando! ma non troppo, ppp."

He gave them money, more than they could count,
Scent, from a most ingenious little fount,
    More beer, in little kegs,
    Many dozen hard-boiled eggs,
And goodies to a fabulous amount.

53

Now follows the dim horror of my tale,
And I feel I'm growing gradually pale,
  For, even at this day,
  Though its sting has passed away,
When I venture to remember it, I quail!

The elder of the brothers gave a squeal,
All-overish it made me for to feel!
  "Oh, Prince," he says, says he,
  "If a Prince indeed you be,
I've a mystery I'm going to reveal!

"Oh, listen, if you'd shun a horrid death,
To what the gent who's speaking to you, saith:
  No 'Oüiats' in truth are we,
  As you fancy that we be,
For (ter-remble!) I am Aleck—this is Beth!"

Said Agib, "Oh! accursed of your kind,
I have heard that ye are men of evil mind!"
  Beth gave a dreadful shriek—
  But before he'd time to speak
I was mercilessly collared from behind.

In number ten or twelve, or even more,
They fastened me, full length upon the floor.
  On my face extended flat
  I was walloped with a cat,
For listening at the keyhole of the door.

Oh! the horror of that agonizing thrill!
(I can feel the place in frosty weather still).
  For a week from ten to four
  I was fastened to the floor,
While a mercenary wopped me with a will!

They branded me, and broke me on a wheel,
And they left me in an hospital to heal;
  And, upon my solemn word,
  I have never, never heard
What those Tartars had determined to reveal.

But that day of sorrow, misery, and rage,
I shall carry to the Catacombs of Age,
  Photographically lined
  On the tablet of my mind,
When a yesterday has faded from its page!

William S. Gilbert

Ferdinando and Elvira

or The Gentle Pieman

Part I

At a pleasant evening party I had taken down to
  supper
One whom I will call Elvira, and we talked of love
  and Tupper.

Mr. Tupper and the poets, very lightly with them
  dealing,
For I've always been distinguished for a strong
  poetic feeling.

Then we let off paper crackers, each of which con-
  tained a motto,
And she listened while I read them, till her mother
  told her not to.

Then she whispered, "To the ball-room we had bet-
  ter, dear, be walking;
If we stop down here much longer, really people
  will be talking."

There were noblemen in coronets, and military
  cousins,

There were captains by the hundred, there were
    baronets by dozens.

Yet she heeded not their offers, but dismissed them
    with a blessing;
Then she let down all her back-hair which had
    taken long in dressing.

Then she had convulsive sobbings in her agitated
    throttle,
Then she wiped her pretty eyes and smelt her pretty
    smelling bottle.

So I whispered, "Dear Elvira, say,—what can the
    matter be with you?
Does anything you've eaten, darling Popsy, dis-
    agree with you?"

But spite of all I said, her sobs grew more and
    more distressing,
And she tore her pretty back-hair, which had taken
    long in dressing.

Then she gazed upon the carpet, at the ceiling then
    above me,
And she whispered, "Ferdinando, do you really,
    really love me?"

"Love you?" said I, then I sighed, and then I gazed
   upon her sweetly—
For I think I do this sort of thing particularly
   neatly—

"Send me to the Arctic regions, or illimitable azure,
On a scientific goose-chase, with my Coxwell or
   my Glaisher!

"Tell me whither I may hie me, tell me, dear one,
   that I may know—
Is it up the highest Andes? down a horrible vol-
   cano?"

But she said, "It isn't polar bears, or hot volcanic
   grottoes,
Only find out who it is that writes those lovely
   cracker mottoes!"

Part II

"Tell me, Henry Wadsworth, Alfred, Poet Close, or
   Mister Tupper,
Do you write the bonbon mottoes my Elvira pulls
   at supper?"

But Henry Wadsworth smiled, and said he had not
   had that honor:

60

And Alfred, too, disclaimed the words that told so
much upon her.

"Mister Martin Tupper, Poet Close, I beg of you
inform us";
But my question seemed to throw them both into a
rage enormous.

Mister Close expressed a wish that he could only get
anigh to me,
And Mister Martin Tupper sent the following reply
to me:—

"A fool is bent upon a twig, but wise men dread a
bandit,"
Which I know was very clever; but I didn't under-
stand it.

Seven weary years I wandered—Patagonia, China,
Norway,
Till at last I sank exhausted at a pastrycook his
doorway.

There were fuchsias and geraniums, and daffodils
and myrtle,
So I entered, and I ordered half a basin of mock
turtle.

He was plump and he was chubby, he was smooth
and he was rosy,
And his little wife was pretty, and particularly cozy.

And he chirped and sang, and skipped about, and
laughed with laughter hearty—
He was wonderfully active for so very stout a party.

And I said, "Oh, gentle pieman, why so very, very
merry?
Is it purity of conscience, or your one-and-seven
sherry?"

But he answered, "I'm so happy—no profession
could be dearer—
If I am not humming 'Tra! la! la!' I'm singing
'Tirer, lirer!'

"First I go and make the patties, and the puddings
and the jellies,
Then I make a sugar birdcage, which upon a table
swell is;

"Then I polish all the silver, which a supper-table
lacquers;
Then I write the pretty mottoes which you find
inside the crackers"—

"Found at last!" I madly shouted.   "Gentle pieman,
    you astound me!"
Then I waved the turtle soup enthusiastically
    round me.

And I shouted and I danced until he'd quite a
    crowd around him—
And I rushed away exclaiming, "I have found him!
    I have found him!"

And I heard the gentle pieman in the road behind
    me trilling,
" 'Tira! lira!' stop him, stop him! 'Tra! la! la!' the
    soup's a shilling!"

But until I reached Elvira's home, I never, never
    waited,
And Elvira to her Ferdinand 's irrevocably mated!

                                    William S. Gilbert

Eugene Field and James Whitcomb Riley are not remembered for their nonsense but for their rhymes about childhood and for children. But there must be a little of their rollicking fun here, if only to suggest to any reader that he must get to know them better. And with them is placed Charles E. Carryl whose "Davy and the Goblin" belongs on the same book-shelf with the Alice books.

The Little Peach

A little peach in the orchard grew,
A little peach of emerald hue;
Warmed by the sun and wet by the dew,
 It grew.

One day, passing that orchard through,
That little peach dawned on the view
Of Johnny Jones and his sister Sue,
 Them two.

Up at that peach a club they threw,
Down from the stem on which it grew
Fell that peach of emerald hue.
 Mon Dieu!

John took a bite and Sue took a chew,
And then the trouble began to brew,

Trouble the doctor couldn't subdue.
    Too true!

Under the turf where the daisies grew
They planted John and his sister Sue,
And their little souls to the angels flew,
    Boo hoo!

What of that peach of the emerald hue;
Warmed by the sun and wet by the dew?
Ah, well, its mission on earth is through.
    Adieu!

Eugene Field

The Dinkey-Bird

In an ocean, 'way out yonder
    (As all sapient people know),
Is the land of Wonder-Wander,
    Whither children love to go;
It's their playing, romping, swinging,
    That give great joy to me
While the Dinkey-Bird goes singing
    In the Amfalula-tree!

There the gum-drops grow like cherries,
    And taffy's thick as peas,—

Caramels you pick like berries
  When, and where, and how you please:
Big red sugar-plums are clinging
  To the cliffs beside that sea
Where the Dinkey-Bird is singing
  In the Amfalula-tree.

So when children shout and scamper
  And make merry all the day,
When there's naught to put a damper
  To the ardor of their play;
When I hear their laughter ringing
  Then I'm sure as sure can be
That the Dinkey-Bird is singing
  In the Amfalula-tree.

For the Dinkey-Bird's bravuras
  And staccatos are so sweet—
His rolades, appogiaturas,
  And robustos so complete,
That the youth of every nation—
  Be they near or far away—
Have especial delectation
  In that gladsome roundelay.

Their eyes grow bright and brighter,
  Their lungs begin to crow;

Their hearts get light and lighter,
  And their cheeks are all aglow;
For an echo cometh bringing
  The news to all and me,
That the Dinkey-Bird is singing
  In the Amfalula-tree.

I'm sure you'd like to go there
  To see your feathered friend—
And so many goodies grow there
  You would like to comprehend!
Speed, little dreams, your winging
  To that land across the sea
Where the Dinkey-Bird is singing
  In the Amfalula-Tree!

Eugene Field

The Spirk Troll-Derisive

The Crankadox leaned o'er the edge of the moon
  And wistfully gazed on the sea
Where the Gryxabodill madly whistled a tune
  To the air of "Ti-fol-de-ding-dee."
The quavering shriek of the Fliupthecreek
  Was fitfully wafted afar

To the Queen of the Wunks as she powdered her
    cheek
  With the pulverized rays of a star.

The Gool closed his ear on the voice of the Grig,
  And his heart it grew heavy as lead
As he marked the Baldekin adjusting his wig
  On the opposite side of his head;
And the air it grew chill as the Gryxabodill
  Raised his dank, dripping fins to the skies
To plead with the Plunk for the use of her bill
  To pick the tears out of his eyes.

The ghost of the Zhack flitted by in a trance;
  And the Squidjum hid under a tub
As he heard the loud hooves of the Hooken advance
  With a rub-a-dub-dub-a-dub dub!
And the Crankadox cried as he laid down and died,
  "My fate there is none to bewail!"
While the Queen of the Wunks drifted over the tide
  With a long piece of crape to her tail.

                                    James Whitcomb Riley

An Alphabet

Have Angleworms attractive homes?
Do Bumble Bees have brains?
Do Caterpillars carry combs?

Do Dodos dote on drains?
Can Eels elude elastic earls?
Do Flatfish fish for flats?
Are Grigs agreeable to girls?
Do Hares have hunting hats?
Do Ices make an Ibex ill?
Do Jackdaws jug their jam?
Do Kites kiss all the kids they kill?
Do Llamas live on lamb?
Will Moles molest a mounted Mink?
Do Newts deny the news?
Are Oysters boisterous when they drink?
Do Parrots prowl in pews?
Do Quakers get their quills from quails?
Do Rabbits rob on roads?
Are Snakes supposed to sneer at snails?
Do Tortoises tease toads?
Can Unicorns perform on horns?
Do Vipers value veal?
Do Weasels weep when fast asleep?
Can Xylophagans squeal?
Do Yaks in packs invite attacks?
Are Zebras full of zeal?

Charles E. Carryl

The Walloping Window-Blind

A capital ship for an ocean trip
    Was the "Walloping Window-blind"—
No gale that blew dismayed her crew
    Or troubled the captain's mind.
The man at the wheel was taught to feel
    Contempt for the wildest blow,
And it often appeared, when the weather had
    cleared,
    That he'd been in his bunk below.

The boatswain's mate was very sedate,
    Yet fond of amusement, too;
And he played hop-scotch with the starboard watch,
    While the captain tickled the crew.
And the gunner we had was apparently mad,
    For he sat on the after rail,
And fired salutes with the captain's boots,
    In the teeth of the booming gale.

The captain sat in a commodore's hat
    And dined in a royal way
On toasted pigs and pickles and figs
    And gummery bread each day.
But the cook was Dutch and behaved as such:
    For the food that he gave the crew

Was a number of tons of hot-cross buns
  Chopped up with sugar and glue.

And we all felt ill as mariners will,
  On a diet that's cheap and rude;
And we shivered and shook as we dipped the cook
  In a tub of his gluesome food.
Then nautical pride we laid aside,
  And we cast the vessel ashore
On the Gulliby Isles, where the Poohpooh smiles,
  And the Anagazanders roar.

Composed of sand was that favored land,
  And trimmed with cinnamon straws;
And pink and blue was the pleasing hue
  Of the Tickletoeteaser's claws.
And we sat on the edge of a sandy ledge
  And shot at the whistling bee;
And the Binnacle-bats wore water-proof hats
  As they danced in the sounding sea.

On rubagub bark, from dawn to dark,
  We fed, till we all had grown
Uncommonly shrunk,—when a Chinese junk
  Came by from the torriby zone.
She was stubby and square, but we didn't much
    care;
  And we cheerily put to sea;

And we left the crew of the junk to chew
The bark of the rubagub tree.

Charles E. Carryl

Oliver Herford, Gelett Burgess and Carolyn Wells are still writing. Long may they continue. They have done much to keep a rightful place for nonsense in today's literature, the first by his many books and pictures, the second by his "Nonsense Book" and "The Lark," a little magazine in which "The Purple Cow" and the Goops first appeared; and the third by her "Nonsense Anthology" which brought together, for the first time, a wonderful collection.

The Hen

Alas! my Child, where is the Pen
That can do justice to the Hen?
Like Royalty, She goes her way,
Laying foundations every day,
Though not for Public Buildings, yet
For Custard, Cake, and Omelette.
Or if too old for such a use,
They have their Fling at some Abuse
As when to Censure Plays Unfit
Upon the Stage they make a Hit,
Or at elections Seal the Fate
Of an Obnoxious Candidate.
No wonder, Child, we prize the Hen
Whose Egg is Mightier than the Pen.

Oliver Herford

The Ant

My child, ob-serve the use-ful Ant,
  How hard she works each day;
She works as hard as ad-a-mant
  (That's very hard, they say).
She has no time to gal-li-vant;
  She has no time to play.
Let Fi-do chase his tail all day;
  Let Kit-ty play at tag;
She has no time to throw away,
  She has no tail to wag;
She hur-ries round from morn till night;
  She nev-er, nev-er sleeps;
She seiz-es ev-er-y thing in sight,
She drags it home with all her might,
  And all she takes she keeps.

The Chimpanzee

Children, behold the Chimpanzee:
He sits on the ancestral tree
From which we sprang in ages gone.
I'm glad we sprang: had we held on,
We might, for aught that I can say,
Be horrid Chimpanzees to-day.

Oliver Herford

77

The Purple Cow

I never saw a Purple Cow,
  I never hope to see one;
But I can tell you, anyhow,
  I'd rather see than be one.

Gelett Burgess

My Legs Are So Weary

My Legs are so Weary
They Break Off in Bed;
And my Caramel Pillow
It Sticks to my Head!

Gelett Burgess

I'd Rather Have Fingers Than Toes

I'd rather have Fingers than Toes;
I'd rather have Ears than a Nose;
  And as for my Hair,
   I'm glad it's All There;
I'll be Awfully Sad when it Goes!

Gelett Burgess

A Tutor Who Tooted the Flute

A tutor who tooted the flute
Tried to tutor two tooters to toot.
  Said the two to the tutor,
  "Is it harder to toot or
To tutor two tooters to toot?"

                      Carolyn Wells

One Week

The year had gloomily begun
For Willie Weeks, a poor man's
                SUN.

He was beset with bill and dun,
And he had very little
                MON.

"This cash," said he, "won't pay my dues,
I've nothing here but ones and
                TUES."

A bright thought struck him, and he said
"The rich Miss Goldrocks I will
                WED."

But when he paid his court to her,
She lisped, but plainly said, "No,
                              THUR.!"

"Alas!" said he, "then I must die!"
His soul went where they say souls
                              FRI.

They found his gloves, and coat, and hat;
The Coroner upon them
                              SAT.
                                   Carolyn Wells